31 Day Novena
to

St. Joseph

Edited by Dr. Rosalie A. Turton

+++

First printing: September, 2001
20,000 copies
Printed in the U.S.A.

This booklet is available from:
The 101 Foundation, Inc.
P.O. Box 151
Asbury, NJ 08802-0151
Phone: 908-689 8792
Fax: 908-689 1957
www.101foundation.com
email: 101@101foundation.com

ISBN: 1-890137-51-0

HAIL, BLESSED JOSEPH!

31 Day Novena
to
St. Joseph

This novena is based on the powerful, beautiful, indulgenced, and efficatious *Litany of St. Joseph*. The novena need not be said on 31 consecutive days, but it is recommended that it be completed in no more than 40 days, in honor of the fasting of the God-Man, Jesus, the Son of Joseph.

For 31 days, an intention for yourself or for someone else, should be thought of every day during the novena. If your petition is expeditiously granted (and in God's time it will be, if it is for the good of souls) it is recommended that another 31 day novena be said in thanksgiving.

Daily prayers and meditations are taken from the book, *St. Joseph, As Seen By Mystics And Historians*, available from the 101 Foundation, Inc.

Prayer for Each Day:

(To be said prior to the daily novena prayer.)

(For the intention of _____)

Dear Father St. Joseph, you are the virginal father of Jesus, as Mary was His virginal mother. I call Her my mother, and so it is fitting to call you my father.

St. Teresa of Avila said: "The Lord wants us to understand that just as He was subject to St. Joseph on earth—for since bearing the title of father, being the Lord's tutor, Joseph could give the Child commands—so in Heaven, God does whatever Joseph commands...

"To the other saints, God gives the grace to help us in certain particular needs, but to Saint Joseph, He gives power to help us in *all* our needs."

Dear Father St. Joseph, your life teaches us that true greatness consists in serving God and our neighbor, and that the really thrilling exploits are the conscientious and loving accomplishment of one's duties, no matter how humble.

Saint Joseph constantly said: "My God, I love you. Help me with the grace to perform this action according to Your divine good pleasure."

Dear Father St. Joseph, assist me, like you, to repeat this prayer throughout the day, so that, like you, I may spend my day in perpetual prayer.

Dear Father St. Joseph, you continuously exercise your intermediary function before God on behalf of the dying. You manifest a deep concern for the welfare of all souls redeemed by the Precious Blood of the Savior. You obtain graces for all, but you manifest a special solicitude for those who honor you.

Dear Father St. Joseph, pray and intercede for me that God may swiftly grant my request. +++

FIRST DAY

St. Joseph

They say the word "Joseph," means "to increase." Dear Father St. Joseph, each day you increased your merits and your love for God the Father, God the Son, God the Holy Spirit, and later, the Blessed Ever Virgin Mary. After your death, this enabled you to go to the highest place in Heaven, next to Mary, the Mother of God.

It is not selfish of me to want to go to a higher place in Heaven. It is rather God's Own desire, yours, and that of all the saints. Therefore, dear Father St. Joseph, assist me to be like you, and to "increase" each day in my merits and love for God so that for all eternity I may experience the joy of being closer to God, to Our Lady, and to you and all the saints.

Let me not be content with mediocre efforts, or a desire just to "make it" into Purgatory. Let me say, with St. Therese, *The Little Flower*, "I want it all!" Help me to reach greater heights of holiness than those to which I am now capable of achieving, but with your all-powerful intercession they become readily attainable.

Dear Father St. Joseph, never cease recommending me, and the intention of this novena, to your Divine Son and your most Holy Spouse, Who are ever ready to grant your requests. +++

SECOND DAY

Renowned Offspring of David

The descendants of David were respected as members of the first family in the land, and their pedigrees were kept as faithfully as in the days of their greatness, for the people knew that the Messiah was to be born of their stock.

3.

The title, "Son of David," was held in honor all over Israel. The blood of David ennobled all his descendants, no matter how low their fortunes had fallen, and Israel held them in higher honor than even its priests of the proud House of Aaron.

Joseph descended from 14 patriarchs after Abraham, from 14 kings after David, and from 14 princes or chiefs of the people. He was the *chief representative* of the royal line of David.

Joseph had an exalted intellect, his judgment was profound, and his wisdom surpassed that of the wisest among men. After Jesus Himself, no other man was gifted with greater nobility or virtues.

As many light-years away in quality as Joseph was from the Ever Virgin Mary, all other men were many light-years away from the dignity and nobility of Joseph. No other man born of a woman could possibly have been the spouse of that pure and exalted Maiden, created to be the Mother of God.

Such is the dignity and incomparability of St. Joseph. So, too, are his powers and influence in Heaven.

Dear Father St. Joseph, never cease recommending me, and the intention of this novena, to your Divine Son and your most Holy Spouse, Who are ever ready to grant your requests. +++

THIRD DAY

Light of Patriarchs

Like the Patriarch Joseph of Egypt, St. Joseph, the husband of Mary, was handsome. St. Joseph was of noble lineage, a most perfect soul, created to be the spouse of the most beautiful Woman of all women, the culmination and the last of the Old Testament patriarchs, most of whom were extremely handsome, such as Abraham, Jacob, Joseph, David, Solomon, and so on.

But of all the patriarchs, he was the "light," the brightest, the most perfect of men...for we see how Saint Joseph's genealogy is most glorious and how God privileged him to become most worthy of whatever was to follow, for his lineage was foretold to be messianic.

Why must we think that St. Joseph was ugly? Usually the most handsome are always those of noble descent, and the most perfect should have dominion over their faculties and passions.

Being of the finest ancestry in the world, Joseph was born into poverty. Since Joseph was of noble descent, he was not born with a natural inclination to manual labor, but he did *all* things according to the divine good pleasure of God.

Dear Father St. Joseph, never cease recommending me, and the intention of this novena, to your Divine Son and your most Holy Spouse, Who are ever ready to grant your requests. +++

FOURTH DAY

Spouse of the Mother of God

The virginal marriage of Mary and Joseph was only contracted on earth after having been decided in Heaven, and these two spouses were perfectly worthy One of the other. Mary surpassed all men and angels in the sovereign plenitude of Her graces; therefore, it was necessary that, after Her, Joseph should be the most holy human being that existed, that had ever existed, or that should ever exist upon earth.

According to the ancient law, whoever espouses a queen becomes a king by the fact of his marriage. From this, we can draw the conclusion: Mary is Queen of Angels and of Saints; Joseph is the spouse of Mary, therefore, he is also King of Angels and Saints.

7.

Pere Lamy said, "St. Joseph is not just a simple working man, as they are too much inclined to depict him. That is only one side of this holy personage, but he was very well versed in the Psalms and knew the Holy Scripture. He was a cultured man, fit to live in the company of the Blessed Virgin, and he understood Her. He was of one mind with Her."

Dear Father St. Joseph, never cease recommending me, and the intention of this novena, to your Divine Son and most Holy Spouse, Who are ever ready to grant your requests. +++

FIFTH DAY

Chaste Guardian of the Virgin

In the virtue and perfection of chastity, St. Joseph was elevated higher than the Seraphim; for the purity, which they possessed without a body, he possessed in his earthly body and in mortal flesh; never did an image of the impurities of the animal and sensible natures engage, even for one moment, any of his faculties.

This freedom from all such imaginations and his angelic simplicity fitted him for the companionship and presence of the most Pure among all creatures, and without this excellence, he would not have been worthy of so great a dignity and rare excellence.

At tender ages, inspired by God and knowing that it was His pleasure, both Holy Mary and St. Joseph had taken private vows of chastity. Later, when they knew that it was God's will for them to marry, so great was their love and devotion to virginity, that they made no account of the disgrace, as it was thought, of infecundity, and cared not for the reproach it would bring upon them.

Others hastened to contract marriage, at the sacrifice of their virginity, with the hope of having the Messiah born to their race, while these two holy spouses, on the contrary had made a vow of perpetual virginity, reputing themselves unworthy of that honor; and lo! It was they to whom the Messiah would be given without loss of their angelic purity.

They had hidden it, heedless of what men would think on beholding them childless. But God delivered the humble from the contempt of the proud, and to these virgin spouses, divinely conceded a Son, the fairest and the most exalted among the children of men.

While St. Joseph's extraordinary chastity is due chiefly to God's singular grace, yet we must not fail to give credit to the saint for corresponding with this grace. His great chastity was the fruit of continual vigilance on his part.

St. Joseph continually watched over his mind, his heart, his senses; he was careful to avoid idleness, which is the root of all evil; to avoid worldly pleasures and amusements; to avoid bad company, bad conversations, everything that could be an occasion of sin. And knowing that chastity depends on prayer, he never ceased to implore God's help and God's grace.

Dear Father St. Joseph, never cease recommending me, and the intention of this novena, to your Divine Son and your most Holy Spouse, Who are ever ready to grant your requests. +++

SIXTH DAY

Foster Father of the Son of God

In a revelation by Our Lady to St. Bridget of Sweden, the Blessed Mother said: "From the moment I gave My consent to God's messenger, then Joseph, seeing that, having conceived by the power of the Holy Spirit, I was pregnant and that I was growing, wondered greatly.

"Because he would not suspect evil but remembered the words of the prophet who foretold that the Son of God would be born of a Virgin, he reputed himself unworthy to serve such a Mother, until the angel in a dream commanded him not to fear but to minister to Me with charity."

Oh inestimable tribute to Mary. Joseph believed in Her chastity more than in Her womb... in grace more than in nature! He plainly saw the conception, and he was incapable of suspecting evil. He believed that it was more possible for a virgin to conceive and remain a virgin, than for Mary to be able to sin.

While Joseph was not Christ's natural father but rather his putative father with regard to generation, he was much more than a putative father, much more than an adoptive father, and much more than a foster father. He was Christ's father in every way except by generation.

He was His true father by affection, by care and solicitude, by education, by authority, by right of marriage, by right of naming Him, and by appointment as such by God Himself. And Joseph was loved, honored, and obeyed by Jesus Christ as His true father.

Dear Father St. Joseph, never cease recommending me, and the intention of this novena, to your Divine Son and your most Holy Spouse, Who are ever ready to grant your requests. +++

SEVENTH DAY

Diligent Protector of Christ

While all men would contribute to the death of the Savior, only one, St. Joseph, was to save Him from death in His infancy. Crisis reveals character. The flight into Egypt now showed to Mary that God had given Her not only a devoted lover and a loyal husband, but a resolute man of action who would shirk nothing in Her defense and that of the Child.

Let us consider now the anxiety and fright that Joseph suffered at the time when King Herod was looking for the Child to kill Him. Joseph was so unprepared for this news that, according to the Armenians, he fled the city as soon as he could with his Wife and left Her hidden in a cave. Then he went back to the city to look for some provisions and things for the journey, and he was an eyewitness to the slaughter of the Holy Innocents.

Afterwards, St. Joseph returned from the city with a few things for such a long journey, filled with fear and fright, and with this anxiety, the Holy Family began its flight from King Herod. And, since Joseph was afraid that they would be overtaken, he became uneasy when he saw soldiers on the road, fearful that they would tear the Child from Mary's arms, as he had seen them do to others in the city.

The fear of being overtaken and discovered always accompanied those who fled, and made this journey for them a continuous nightmare, and Jerusalem was less than two hours away from Bethlehem. The flight was a rough one six or seven days long.

In order to go to Egypt, they traveled through the desert and through towns. In the desert, they had to be on the watch for tigers, lions, snakes, beasts, wild animals, and robbers. The towns were inhabited by Gentiles, who were archenemies of the Israelites; since Joseph did not carry a halbred (weapon), he could not be sure of anything...and all this in the hardest part of winter with the discomfort of wind and snow!

In order to furnish Them with some kind of shelter against the open air, however narrow and humble it might be, St. Joseph formed a sort of tent for the Divine Word and most Holy Mary by means of his cloak and some sticks. Everything they needed was lacking.

Another way that Joseph protected the God-man which also required tremendous strength, was to keep life-long silence about the Christ Child, in order more fittingly to hide from any witnesses the wonders which passed between them, and which were not to be communicated to outsiders. In silence, he prayed for many, and obtained the intercession of the Christ Child and His Mother.

Dear Father St. Joseph, never cease recommending me, and the intention of this novena, to your Divine Son and your most Holy Spouse, Who are ever ready to grant your requests. +++

EIGHTH DAY

Head of the Holy Family

Joseph was a king in the little home of Nazareth, for he sheltered within it the Prince of Peace and the Queen of Heaven. To him, They looked for protection and sustenance, and Joseph did not fail Them. He received from Them the deepest love and reverence, and in him They saw Him, Whose place he took over Them.

St. Francis de Sales states: "If earthly princes consider it a matter of so much importance to select carefully a tutor fit for their children, think you that the Eternal God would not, in His almighty power and wisdom, choose from out of His creation the most perfect man living to be the guardian of His divine and most glorious Son, the Prince of Heaven and earth?

"There is, then, no doubt at all that Saint Joseph was endowed with all gifts and graces required by the charge which the Eternal Father willed to commit to him, over all the domestic and temporal concerns of our Lord, and the guidance of St. Joseph's family, which was composed of three persons only, representing to us the mystery of the most Holy and Adorable Trinity.

"Not that there is any real comparison in this matter, excepting as regards our Lord, Who is One of the Persons of the most Blessed Trinity, for the others were but creatures; yet still we may say that it was a trinity on earth representing in some sort the most Holy Trinity, Mary, Jesus, and Joseph—Joseph, Jesus, and Mary—a trinity worthy to be honored and greatly esteemed!

St. Joseph shows all of us how to be servants of the Word rather than be masters over others. His hidden and silent oblation of self can serve as an antidote to a self-seeking generation.

Pope John Paul II sums up the existence of Joseph's magnanimity with regard to the Holy Family in these words: "Joseph surrendered his whole existence to the demands of the Messiah's coming into his home."

How can we sufficiently admire the unremitting, uncomplaining, self-sacrificing toil of Joseph, who was honored by the Eternal Father with the office of governing and working for His Eternal Son and the ever-blessed Virgin Mother.

Dear Father St. Joseph, never cease recommending me, and the intention of this novena, to your Divine Son and your most Holy Spouse, Who are ever ready to grant your requests. +++

NINTH DAY

Joseph Most Just

Because he was "just," Joseph experienced anxiety over the Blessed Mother's pregnancy. He was anxious to obey the Law.

To a Jew, the word "just" means one who is a careful observer of the Law. To be just is simply to be in perfect union with the will of God and to conform to it in all events, in prosperity or adversity. No one can doubt that St. Joseph was perfectly obedient to God at all times and occasions.

As Abraham was prepared to sacrifice Isaac, who was most dear to him, because of the signified (clearly indicated) will of God, so Joseph was similarly concerned with responding to the will of God as he understood that will during the time of his doubt. This was not a theoretical question, but a real existential spiritual trial that Joseph, the "just man," underwent.

And, how could Joseph be called "just," if he concealed his Wife's crime? The truth is that his silence is a witness of Mary's innocence, for Joseph, knowing Her chastity and at the same time astonished at what had taken place, conceals by his silence the mystery which had not been made known to him.

Joseph as a just man, in the first place, could not treat as guilty One Whom he firmly believed to be innocent...but it was equally incumbent on him as a just man to refuse to acknowledge as his, a Child of another.

St. Bernard said, "In order not to be reduced to telling lies, or to laying an innocent One open to blame, it was quite right of St. Joseph, the just man, to separate from Our Lady in secret."

He would feel this separation more acutely than if his soul had been torn from his body. To lose Mary forever, to never see Her again, to separate himself from Her in this manner, he knew, would cause him to die of a broken heart...but what of that, if avoiding it meant he had to disobey God.

His drastic decision was due solely to his desire to conform with God's holy will and to show his absolute trust in God. May his example ever be before my eyes, that I, like him, may be just, trusting, and concerned only with doing the will of God.

Dear Father St. Joseph, never cease recommending me, and the intention of this novena, to your Divine Son and your most Holy Spouse, Who are ever ready to grant your requests. +++

TENTH DAY

Joseph Most Chaste

Venerable Mary of Agreda tells of this conversation between Mary and Joseph. Our Lady said: "At a tender age, being compelled thereto by the force of this truth, which, with the knowledge of the deceitfulness of visible things His divine light made known to Me, I consecrated Myself to God by a perpetual vow of chastity in body and soul. His I am, and Him I acknowledge as My Spouse and Lord, with fixed resolve to preserve for Him My chastity.

"I beseech thee, in all other things I will be thy servant, willing to work for the comfort of thy life as long as Mine shall last. Yield, My spouse, to this resolve, and make a like resolve, in order that, offering ourselves as an acceptable sacrifice to our eternal God, He may receive us in the odor of sweetness and bestow on us the eternal goods for which we hope."

The most chaste, Joseph, full of interior joy at the words of his Heavenly Spouse, answered Her: "My Mistress, in making known to me Thy chaste and welcome sentiments, Thou hast penetrated and dilated my heart. I have not opened my thoughts to Thee before knowing Thy own.

"I also acknowledge myself under greater obligation to the Lord of Creation than other men; for very early He has called me by His true enlightenment to love Him with an upright heart; and I desire Thee to know, Lady, that at the age of twelve years, I also made a promise to serve the Most High in perpetual chastity.

"On this account I now gladly ratify this vow in order not to impede Thy own. In the presence of His Majesty, I promise to aid Thee, as far as in me lies, in serving Him according to Thy full desires. I will be with the divine grace, Thy most faithful servant and companion, and I pray Thee accept my chaste love and hold me as Thy brother, without ever entertaining any other kind of love, outside the one which Thou owest to God, and after God to me."

In this conversation, the Most High confirmed anew the virtue of chastity in the heart of Saint Joseph, and the pure and holy love due to his most holy Spouse Mary. This love the saint already had in an eminent degree, and the Lady Herself augmented it sweetly, dilating his heart by Her most prudent discourse.

By divine operation, the two most holy and chaste spouses felt an incomparable joy and consolation. The Heavenly Princess, as One Who is the Mistress of all virtues, and Who in all things pursued the highest perfection of all virtues, lovingly corresponded to the desires of Saint Joseph.

The Most High also gave Saint Joseph new purity and complete

command over his natural inclinations, so that without hin-
drance of any trace of sensual
desires, but with admirable and
new grace, he might serve his
Spouse Mary, and in Her, execute
His will and pleasure.

Dear Father St. Joseph, never
cease recommending me, and the
intention of this novena, to your
Divine Son and your most Holy
Spouse, Who are ever ready to
grant your requests. +++

ELEVENTH DAY

Joseph Most Prudent

St. Joseph was incomparable
in modesty and gravity. Even
when very young, he was wise
and prudent and had mature
judgment.

Fr. Jerome Gracian tells us
that Saint Joseph epitomizes
human wholeness—the integration
and harmony of the inner and

outer self; the saint's self-control, discipline, maturity, chastity, wisdom, and prudence are clearly manifested by his gracefulness and attractiveness.

Our Lady knew that in taking a husband, She was taking a superior, a confidant of Her thoughts, a depository of Her secrets, a witness of Her actions. He must, therefore, be eminently prudent, faithful, and chaste; in a word, he must be eminently holy.

During persecution, criticism, disparagement, and unknowing, he remained silent in order not to reveal his secret and to do God's will. His prudence guided him never to be impatient or angry. His constant desire was to do only the will of God. May I daily grow more like St. Joseph.

Dear Father St. Joseph, never cease recommending me, and the intention of this novena, to your Divine Son and your most Holy Spouse, Who are ever ready to grant your requests. +++

TWELFTH DAY

Joseph Most Strong

A person who overcomes strong opponents or obstacles is called "strong." Joseph conquered the devil; he conquered a tyrannical king; he conquered himself, surrendering to the angel when he revealed to him the mystery of the Incarnation; he despised the world, trampling it underfoot; he conquered his appetites and all that is contrary to virtue.

This holy man was an example of fortitude for the martyrs, who, with their eyes fixed on Saint Joseph, had the strength to suffer a thousand deaths not to lose Christ. Joseph must have had a superabundance of all the gifts of the Holy Spirit.

Jesus says to Valtorta: "Was Joseph not on Golgatha? Do you think he is not amongst the co-redeemers? I tell you solemnly that he was the first, and, therefore, he is great in the eyes of God. Great for his sacrifice, his patience, his perseverance, his faith. Which faith is greater than this one that believed without seeing the miracles of the Messiah?

"Praise be to My putative father, an example to you of what you lack most: purity, faithfulness, and perfect love. Praise be to that magnificent reader of the Sealed Book of the Immaculate Virgin, imbued with Wisdom to be able to understand the mysteries of Grace, and chosen to protect the Salvation of the World from the snares of all enemies."

With strength, St. Joseph bore the storm of trials, testing and making him a coadjutor of God.

Dear Father St. Joseph, never cease recommending me, and the intention of this novena, to your Divine Son and your most Holy Spouse, Who are ever ready to grant your requests. +++

THIRTEENTH DAY

Joseph Most Obedient

St. Joseph obeyed promptly and without delay. He did not go on sleeping until morning. He did not stay in bed the rest of the night. He got up at once, made known to his Holy Spouse the revelation he had received from the angel and, without delay, taking nothing with them, they departed. Thus they were on their way before dawn, perfectly carrying out the command they were given to flee in secret, as the shades of night permitted them to do.

When Joseph first learned from God's heavenly messenger of the mystery of the Incarnation of the Christ Child by the Holy Spirit that had occurred in the womb of the Blessed Virgin Mary, he forsook what he intended to do and immediately did as the angel commanded.

The primary consecration of Joseph to the good pleasure of His Creator, to do whatever God wished, whether or not Joseph knew what that office was to be, was the essence of that fiat of Joseph to God.

O Almighty God, Who gave to Mary and Joseph a spirit of such perfect obedience, I beg You through their merits to grant me the same spirit, so that I may obey You like them with complete submission of judgment, with courage, promptness, and joy, desiring only to do Your will, and fully confident that Your Divine Providence will never forsake me as long as I shall persevere in uniting my will to Yours.

Dear Father St. Joseph, never cease recommending me, and the intention of this novena, to your Divine Son and your most Holy Spouse, Who are ever ready to grant your requests. +++

FOURTEENTH DAY

Joseph Most Faithful

Saint Joseph was the most faithful and devoted man who ever lived. He wore himself out in the service of Our Lord and of Our Lady in an act of self-devotion whose parallel can be found in no other human being. In this lies his chief accomplishment and his highest praise.

St. Joseph dedicated his whole life to the interests of Jesus. Joseph is an example of faith, righteousness, trust in God's providence, and prompt obedience to God's call.

For Saint Joseph to safeguard Our Lady's virginity under cover of marriage, it was needful that he should be pure as an angel, faithful to chastity, so that his virtue could in some sort correspond to the purity of his Maiden Bride.

To protect the Savior Jesus amid the dangers of His Childhood, it was needful that Joseph should be immovably faithful, with a faithfulness that could not be shaken by the threat of any adversity.

To cherish the secret entrusted to him, it was needful that Joseph should be faithful to humility, avoiding the public gaze, withholding himself from the world, loving to be hidden with Christ Jesus.

If Elizabeth said of the Redeemer's Mother, "Blessed is She who believed," in a certain sense this blessedness can be referred to Saint Joseph as well, since he responded positively to the word of God in complete faith, when it was communicated to him at the decisive moment.

Dear Father St. Joseph, never cease recommending me, and the intention of this novena, to your Divine Son and your most Holy Spouse, who are ever ready to grant your requests. +++

FIFTEENTH DAY

Mirror of Patience

The Holy Family endured all things with invincible patience. Joseph had recourse to Jesus asking: "Oh my precious, beloved Son! Is it really possible that trials are repeatedly to break in upon us, for I behold fresh oppressions arising?"

Jesus reminded Joseph that it was not the time for rest and consolation; moreover, that it was most appropriate to always have some trial to bear. Only in the heavenly homeland could he expect full consolation.

God the Father ordained there always be some affliction for St. Joseph during his life here on earth, in order to prove his fidelity and love. Due to his complete abandonment to the divine will, he accepted with equal readiness and patience, either consolations or tribulations. His countenance always bore a peaceful and contented expression.

By divine revelation, Joseph knew that the Savior would have much to suffer and would finally have to die to complete the work of mankind's redemption. He was grievously saddened by this knowledge, but he also rejoiced exceedingly to have been chosen to live in the Holy Company of Jesus and Mary.

It was Joseph's policy to be content with whatever recompense each customer freely offered to him for his work. No complaint ever fell from his lips, even though some thoughtless individuals gave him little. Then he retained for himself only as much of his earnings as was necessary for their livelihood; the rest he distributed to the poor.

When St. Joseph was in his last illness, God wished to test Joseph's faithfulness to an even greater extent by now permitting the devil again to tempt him. Upon being subjected to an attack of most excruciating pain, he was at the same time seriously tempted to impatience and despair. He defeated the enemy by his undaunted courage and by exciting in himself acts of confidence in God, even when it seemed to him that God had forsaken him.

Dear Father St. Joseph, never cease recommending me, and the intention of this novena, to your Divine Son and your most Holy Spouse, Who are ever ready to grant your requests. +++

SIXTEENTH DAY

Lover of Poverty

The Pseudo-Bonaventure extols poverty as "the highest virtue... the heavenly pearl for which it appears one must exchange everything," and "the main foundation of the whole spiritual edifice." It is the hallmark of the Holy Family's life: "Saintly poverty shines in them, guiding us to love and follow it."

From humility and love of poverty, more than from any absolute necessity, Joseph, the lineal descendant of kings, had subjected himself to the daily toil of a mechanic, which, although it in no way degraded him in the eyes of true Hebrews, placed him in a position of some social inferiority.

Joseph asked the Blessed Virgin: "Is it possible that in Thy most chaste arms I shall see my God and Redeemer? Would that I possessed the richest palaces for His entertainment and many treasures to offer Him."

And, the Sovereign Queen answered: "This great God and Lord does not wish to enter into the world in the pomp of ostentatious riches and royal majesty. He has need of none of these (Ps. 15:2), nor does He come from Heaven for such vanities. He comes to redeem the world and to guide men on the path of eternal life (John 10:10); and this is to be done by means of humility and poverty; in these He wishes to be born, live, and die, in order to destroy in the hearts of men the fetters of covetousness and pride, which keep them from blessedness. He comes to establish truth and to enhance worthily the value of labor.

"On this account He chose our poor and humble house, and desired us not to be rich in apparent, deceitful, and transitory goods, which are but vanity of vanities and affliction of spirit (Eccles. 1:24) and which oppress and obscure the understanding.

"My Son sought destitution and poverty, not because He had any need of them for bringing the practice of virtues to the highest perfection, but in order to teach mortals the shortest and surest way for reaching the heights of divine love and union with God. Let no difficulty or hardship disturb thee, nor deter thee from any virtuous exercise, no matter how hard it may be. Work also for the salvation of souls."

The Blessed Virgin Mary told Saint Bridget, speaking of the poverty in which the Holy Family lived, that: "The surplus from our household, apart from what was necessary for a plain meal, we distributed to the poor, and Joseph served Me with such devotion that I never heard him speak an angry word, nor any vanity nor complaint.

"The fact that we had Jesus with us did not procure us any material wealth. He told us to set our hearts on things of the spirit and ask for His Grace, and that all the rest is unnecessary...that God knows our needs, and will provide for them.

"When we were in fear, poverty, and difficulty, Jesus did not make for us gold and silver, but exhorted us to patience, and we were wonderfully preserved from the envious."

The merit of St. Joseph, then, did not consist in his having been born poor and living a life of poverty, neither was it on this account that God chose him for His representative in the house of His Son on earth, but because he willed and loved to be poor, seeing that God Himself so willed and disposed it.

He was inwardly sensible of the perfection which lay in embracing a life of poverty, even as if he had a prescience that the moment was at hand when voluntary poverty would become one of the most splendid ornaments with which a creature could deck itself in the eyes of its Creator.

Dear Father St. Joseph, never cease recommending me, and the intention of this novena, to your Divine Son and your most Holy Spouse, Who are ever ready to grant your requests. +++

SEVENTEENTH DAY

Model of Artisans

By his life of most faithful fulfillment of daily duty, Saint Joseph left an example to all those who must earn their bread by the work of their hands. He is especially presented as a model of holiness to the class of people that constitutes the overwhelming majority of mankind. He is principal patron in the world of work, for it was as breadwinner of the Holy Family that he plied his trade at Nazareth. In the process, he taught us to sanctify our daily labors, of whatever kind they may be,

Joseph, indeed, was poor, but he was not a beggar because he worked at a trade which implied manual labor, and his state in life should not be regarded as either mean or contemptible. With the

Hebrews, who still retained many of the simple and primitive customs of the Patriarchs, the profession of an artisan, if not noble or distinguished, was yet far from being esteemed as the lowest. The arts were respected as useful to society, and a good artificer was preferred to the richest merchant.

Joseph, the carpenter, who teaches his profession to Jesus, shows the dignity of work, which is measured not by earning power or prestige, but by the love and motivation with which it is done daily.

Certain individuals who were given to idleness, came into Joseph's workshop to talk, only to find themselves completely unnoticed by him. Joseph was characterized as being an inept and feeble-minded person. When this became known, he thanked God that these people considered him to be mentally deficient.

It pleased him, in his humility, not to be esteemed by anyone but to be depreciated. He considered these offenders his benefactors. Nor was he mistaken in his attitude, for this was truly an occasion of great merit for him, and he was able to enrich his soul with imperishable treasures.

St. Joseph was silent, but we must not regret not having any words spoken by him, for the lesson he teaches is precisely the lesson of silence. He knew the Father had confided a secret in trust to him, and the better to keep it so that no slightest inkling of it might leak out, he buried himself in silence. He did not want anyone who saw him to think him other than a simple workman trying to earn his daily bread, so that no sign or word of his might prove an obstacle to the manifestation of the Word.

Saint Joseph still likes to work quietly, and unobstrusively, and because his patronage and charity are universal, all the children of the House of God share in his beneficent influence.

In the blessed repose and peace of Paradise, the Heavenly artisan still labors with supreme energy and consummate skill to realize this dream of beauty—*the likeness of Mary*—in the Church and all Her children. His great work will not be completed until all the predestined partake of Mary's glory in Heaven and, through Her and in Her, of the glory of Jesus, Her Son.

Dear Father St. Joseph, never cease recommending me, and the intention of this novena, to your Divine Son and your most Holy Spouse, Who are ever ready to grant your requests. +++

EIGHTEENTH DAY

Glory of Home Life

St. Joseph's great sanctity is accompanied by no great words or deeds. The details of his life remain lost to history. Jesus' first thirty years belong to the "hidden life" at Nazareth. Joseph teaches us that holiness need not catch the world's attention. It consists, rather, in being lovingly faithful to the ordinary: family, work, religious observance, the indications of circumstances, and God's revelation. Work was the daily expression of love in the life of the Family of Nazareth.

Pope John Paul II tells us, "Through his complete self-sacrifice, Joseph expressed his generous love for the Mother of God, and gave Her a husband's 'gift of self.' Even though he decided to draw back, so as not to interfere in the plan of God which was coming to pass in Mary, Joseph obeyed the explicit command of the angel and took Mary into his home, while respecting the fact that She belonged exclusively to God.

"On the other hand, it was from his marriage to Mary that Joseph derived his singular dignity and his rights in regard to Jesus. It is certain that the dignity of the Mother of God is so exalted that nothing could be more sublime; yet, because Mary was united to Joseph by the bond of marriage, there can be no doubt that Joseph approached, as no other person ever could, the eminent dignity whereby the Mother of God towers above all creatures.

"Since marriage is the highest degree of association and friendship, involving by its very nature a communion of goods, it follows that God, by giving Joseph to the Virgin, did not give him to Her only as a companion for life, a witness of Her virginity and protector of Her honor; He also gave Joseph to Mary in order that he might share, through the marriage pact, in Her own sublime greatness."

Dear Father St. Joseph, never cease recommending me, and the intention of this novena, to your Divine Son and your most Holy Spouse, Who are ever ready to grant your requests. +++

NINETEENTH DAY

Guardian of Virgins

The wisdom of Joseph, the just man, increased by his union and closeness to Mary, Full of Grace, and prepared him to penetrate the deepest secrets of God and enabled him to protect and defend Them from the snares of man and demon. And in the meantime, it invigorated him. It made the just man a saint, and the saint, the guardian of the Spouse and of the Son of God.

St. Teresa of Avila remarked: "I don't know how one can think about the Queen of Angels, and about when She went through so much with the Infant Jesus, without giving thanks to Saint Joseph for the good assistance he then provided to Both of Them.

Jesus said: "As long as I was able to ignore the world because of My age, I did not regret being absent from Paradise. God the Father and the Holy Spirit were not absent, because Mary was Full of Them.

"And the angels dwelt there, because nothing drove them away from that house. And, one of them, I might say, had become flesh and was Joseph, an angelical soul freed from the burden of the flesh, intent only on serving God and His cause, and loving Him as the seraphim love Him. Joseph's look! It was as placid and pure as the brightness of a star unaware of worldly concupiscence. It was our peace, and our strength."

Fr. Jean Jacques Olier, founder of the Society of St. Sulpice, was shown by God that St. Joseph was entrusted with the special care of priests and religious. Thus, St. Joseph was made the patron of their seminary. The Blessed Virgin also gave Saint Joseph to Fr. Olier as a patron, assuring him that Saint Joseph was the guardian of interior souls, and saying: "Outside of My Son, there is no one dearer to Me in Heaven or on earth."

St. Joseph, guardian of virgins, into whose faithful keeping was entrusted Innocence itself, Christ Jesus, and Mary, the Virgin of virgins, I pray and beseech you to keep me from all uncleanness, and to grant that my mind may be untainted, my heart pure, and my body chaste; help me always to serve God in perfect chastity.

Dear Father St. Joseph, never cease recommending me, and the intention of this novena, to your Divine Son and your most Holy Spouse, Who are ever ready to grant your requests. +++

TWENTIETH DAY

Pillar of Families

By nature, offspring need to be provided with three things

from parents: being, nourishment, and education, the neglect of which results in the dissolution of the family. For St. Thomas, it is clear that the rearing of man requires not only the care of the mother, by whom he is nourished, but *even more* the care of the father, who must instruct, defend, and perfect him in both interior and exterior goods.

Jesus grew like a flower protected by vigorous trees, between those two loves that interlaced above Him, to protect Him and love Him. Joseph, then and now, accepts his fatherhood joyfully, and he protects and teaches the entire family of God.

Joseph was the head of the family, and as such, his authority was undisputed; before it, the Spouse and Mother of God bent reverently, and the Son of God submitted Himself willingly. And yet, there was never any abuse of power or a decision against reason. His Spouse was his sweet advisor.

As soon as Jesus was old enough to handle tools, Joseph started Jesus to work and made use of His love of Mary as the means to spur Him to work. Where are now the families in which the little ones are taught to love work as a means of pleasing their parents? A father teaches and protects. Joseph was, and remains, a perfect father.

To the thousands of men deprived of a healthy relationship with their fathers: go to Saint Joseph! To those seeking to overcome a negative father image: seek not further than St. Joseph for a potent cure. To the millions of children in fatherless families: go to Saint Joseph! You will find an earthly father who, like the Heavenly Father, is a father of the fatherless.

Dear Father St. Joseph, never cease recommending me, and the intention of this novena, to your Divine Son and your most Holy Spouse, Who are ever ready to grant your requests. +++

TWENTY-FIRST DAY

Solace of the Wretched

When the Holy Family was told to flee into Egypt, Mary reminded Joseph: "Our Savior has come into this world to suffer, and not to rest. It is a great blessing to be permitted to partake of His sufferings, and we, therefore, should praise and thank Him for it."

The travelers suffered a great deal from hunger and thirst. They frequently had nothing to eat for days. Herbs were to be found only rarely on these plains. Occasionally, they would obtain water to drink in some ravine. The holy wanderers submitted to all this most generously—yes, even with a jubilant heart—because the mere thought that they had their Jesus with them made everything more easily acceptable.

Innkeepers reproached Joseph with being a vagabond, and treated him with derision and rudeness. The saint simply remained silent, and made no excuses for himself. He suffered it all with great patience, offering it all up to God out of love.

Unable to find a place to live, Joseph turned to God and implored Him for aid in his dire necessity. "Oh my God," he prayed, "it has happened that I found no shelter even among relatives and believers. What then can I expect from barbarians and unbelievers? I need Your assistance, oh Lord." And, God heeded his petitions.

The devil, who had been so determined to persecute Joseph and his Spouse, had planned to molest the holy pilgrims as they neared the city. He had already been gloating over the success that he expected from his attacks, only to find himself suddenly disconcerted and completely dismayed by the power which the devil felt being exerted over him.

Joseph endured so much anxiety and distress by reason of his illness and his other trials, and he enriched himself so extensively with merits through the practice of virtue, above all, through his invincible patience, that it now pleases the Most High, as an evidence of His great love for Saint Joseph, to grant all that he asks.

Saint Joseph supplicates for graces on behalf of all men, but particularly for the afflicted and oppressed, since he himself had to endure so much tribulation during his life on earth. Over the centuries, Joseph had shown himself to be an advocate of the world's needy.

Dear Father St. Joseph, never cease recommending me, and the intention of this novena, to your Divine Son and your most Holy Spouse, Who are ever ready to grant your requests. +++

TWENTY-SECOND DAY

Hope of the Sick

St. Teresa of Avila said: "I chose St. Joseph as my advocate and protector. As a tender spiritual father and a loving protector, he quickly cured me of my sickness (while still very young, she was seriously paralyzed) just as he had saved me from greater dangers of other sorts which were menacing my honor and my eternal salvation."

Saint Joseph, although he was not so very old at the time when our Blessed Lady reached Her 33rd year, was much broken and worn out, as far as his body was concerned; for his continual cares, his journeys, and his incessant labors for the sustenance of his Spouse and of the Lord had weakened him much more than his years. This was so ordained by the Lord, Who, wishing to lead him on to the practice of patience and of other virtues, permitted him to suffer sickness and pain.

From that time on, he rested from the hard labor of his hands, by which he had earned a livelihood for all three. They gave away the carpenter tools as an alms, not wishing to have anything superfluous or useless in their house and family. Being thus at leisure, Saint Joseph occupied himself entirely in the contemplation of the mysteries of which he was the guardian and in the exercise of virtues.

As he had the happiness and good fortune of continually enjoying the sight and the intercourse of the Divine Wisdom Incarnate, and of Her, Who was the Mother of It, this man of God reached such a height of sanctity, that (his Heavenly Spouse excepted) no one ever surpassed him, and he far outstripped all other creatures.

The Blessed Lady, and also Her Most Holy Son, attended upon him and nursed him in his sickness, consoling and sustaining him with the greatest assiduity; and hence, there are no words sufficiently expressive of the humility, reverence, and love which all this caused in the simple and grateful heart of this man of God. He thus became the admiration and joy of the angels, and the pleasure and delight of the Most High.

Dear Father St. Joseph, never cease recommending me, and the intention of this novena, to your Divine Son and your most Holy Spouse, Who are ever ready to grant your requests. +++

TWENTY-THIRD DAY

Patron of the Dying

God revealed to Joseph that because of his great concern for the dying throughout his life, assisting them and pleading for their salvation with prayers and tears, He was appointing him as their special mediator and patron, and furthermore, that he wished that he would continue to manifest his love for them until the end of time. From his place in Heaven, he would still be able to exercise this role as special intercessor for all those engaged in the struggle with death.

Jesus says to Saint Joseph: "Because you have lifted your voice to Him, He will hear you; He will be with you in your last affliction; He will glorify you after this life, showing you even now His Salvation. And in the future life, he will let you enter, because of the Savior Who is now comforting you and Who very soon, oh! I repeat it, He will come very soon and hold you in His divine embrace and take you, at the head of all the Patriarchs, where the dwelling place has been prepared for the Just Man of God, who was My blessed father.

"Learn, you who are crying. Learn, you who are dying, Learn you who are living, to die. Endeavor to deserve the words I said to Joseph. They will be your peace in the struggle of death. Learn, you who are dying, to deserve to have Jesus near you, comforting you. And, if you have not deserved it, dare just the same, and call Me near you. I will come with My Hands full of graces and consolation, My Heart full of forgiveness and love. My Lips full of words of absolution and encouragement.

"Death loses its bitterness if it takes place between My Arms. Believe Me, I cannot abolish death, but I can make it sweet for those who die trusting in Me."

Dear Father St. Joseph, never cease recommending me, and the intention of this novena, to your Divine Son and your most Holy Spouse, Who are ever ready to grant your requests. +++

TWENTY-FOURTH DAY

Terror of Demons

Jesus was born of an espoused Mother so that the devil might be deceived, and God willed that the Virgin Mary have a husband for the protection of the Child, lest the devil be particularly vehement against Him. Joseph protected then, as he does now.

St. Joseph particularly has special power over the demons who attack us on our deathbed, this privilege having been given him in recompense for the fact that he preserved the life of Jesus from the impious designs of Herod, and because he has been assigned by God as the special patron of the dying.

God has inspired in demons terror at all times at the mere mention of Saint Joseph's name, for they know well that his power over them is most formidable. The rage and temptations of the devil at that critical moment, when he exerts himself with utmost force to bring souls to the Hell of fire where the worm dieth not, and the fire is never extinguished, is quelled in an instant when Joseph is called upon to intercede.

If a person engages in a lawsuit, on the event of which depends an immense gain or utter ruin, does he not call in the aid of some eminent lawyer, of one whose zeal for his interest he may safely depend? All souls, then, should engage, in a struggle against the demons, St. Joseph, the man God has designated and enabled to conquer them with the greatest efficaciousness.

Dear Father St. Joseph, never cease recommending me, and the intention of this novena, to your Divine Son and your most Holy Spouse, Who are ever ready to grant your requests. +++

TWENTY-FIFTH DAY

Protector of Holy Church

The term "Body of Christ" refers to three interrelated and inseparable realities: the humanity of Christ, the Eucharist, and the Church. By God's design, Joseph is in charge of keeping watch, then and now, over the Body of Christ.

As Mary was from eternity predestined to be the Mother of the Son of God, so also was Joseph elected to be the guardian and protector of Jesus and of Mary. As Joseph protected the physical body of the Child Jesus on earth, so does he continue to protect the mystical body of Christ, the Church.

On December 8, 1870, Saint Joseph was declared the Patron Saint of the Universal Church by Pope Pius IX, who also reinforced March as the month of Saint

Joseph, and who approved the Confraternity of Saint Joseph.

Joseph's fatherly patronage of the Church means his patronage of the entire human race. Since every member of the human race should be fully a member of Christ's Church, and since the Church must strive to bring all humans into union with it, according to its delegation received from Christ, therefore, Joseph is Patron of all the human race.

Dear Father St. Joseph, never cease recommending me, and the intention of this novena, to your Divine Son and your most Holy Spouse, Who are ever ready to grant your requests. +++

TWENTY-SIXTH DAY

Lord Of His Household

For our emulation, we see the example of Joseph in the fact that

Jesus was subject to him...the fact that he who was least in dignity in the Holy Family, was greatest in authority...entrusted by God with authority over the Son of God! Joseph would exercise it with all the respect due to such authority.

Jesus never did anything without Joseph's approval. Jesus did not even leave the shop to go and see His Mother without Joseph's express permission. Joseph was amazed at the Savior's great humility, and endeavored to emulate Him. The sight of Divinity Itself being thus submissive to his commands only made him seek to abase himself all the more.

Hence, when Jesus could not see Joseph do so, he would prostrate himself on the ground and adore Jesus, or when Jesus left the workshop, Joseph would kiss the floor where the Sacred Feet had been standing. Joseph would lovingly put his lips to those articles which his beloved

Son and God had touched with His Sacred Hands.

In that home, there was a pattern of religious observance and of the worship of God. We read in the Holy Scriptures how perfectly our Lord and His parents observed the Law of Moses, even when that Family might have justly claimed to be dispensed from it.

In that home, obedience, self-sacrifice, humility, mortification of the appetites, meekness, chastity, modesty, sobriety—all concurred to its holiness and happiness.

In that home, there was the pattern of charity, piety, and mutual service and kindness... patterns which should be imitated in every Catholic home.

Dear Father St. Joseph, never cease recommending me, and the intention of this novena, to your Divine Son and your most Holy Spouse, Who are ever ready to grant your requests. +++

TWENTY-SEVENTH DAY

Prince Over All His Possessions

When the Patriarch Joseph of Egypt entered any city, all the women ran to the walls and windows to see him pass by, admiring his great handsomeness. He had in his power to dispatch the wealth of Egypt.

When Saint Joseph would enter a place with the Christ Child in his arms, all Heaven would become a window, with the angels in awe at God being carried in the arms of a carpenter. He was a creature who could dispatch the wealth of Heaven!

In their home there was no luxury, and very little comfort was to be found in such dwellings. Straw mats were scattered on the hard earthen floor. The wooden furniture was simple, like that of people round about: bedrolls, clothes chests, household utensils, pitchers, a hand-mill for grinding wheat, a rug or two, and cushions for visitors. But, even on their flight into Egypt, when they left behind them all that they owned, because they had Jesus, Mary and Joseph knew that they had everything.

Joseph is humble; in fact, although he is the guardian of God and of the Mother of God and Spouse of the Most High, he holds the stirrups of these Vassals of God. He is a poor carpenter, because sustained human pressures have deprived David's heirs of their royal wealth. But he is always the offspring of a king, and has the manners of a king. Also, of him it must be said: "He was humble, because he was really great."

Dear Father St. Joseph, never cease recommending me, and the intention of this novena, to your Divine Son and your most Holy Spouse, Who are ever ready to grant your requests. +++

TWENTY-EIGHTH DAY

Chosen Blessed Joseph

There is no doubt that Saint Joseph was more valiant than David and wiser than Solomon, but what must not his wisdom have been, seeing that God committed to his charge His all-glorious Son and chose him to be His guardian.

In the Divine Mind, Joseph was the one chosen from among all others. Joseph held the first place. Joseph was predestined to this office.

True, from the tribe of Juda, from the family of David, great patriarchs were to arise, famous leaders of the people, most noble kings; but God did not choose any of these. He chose Joseph alone. Joseph was the beloved one. Joseph was especially preordained to become one day the happy spouse of Mary and foster-father of Jesus.

Dear Father St. Joseph, never cease recommending me, and the intention of this novena, to your Divine Son and your most Holy Spouse, Who are ever ready to grant your requests. +++

TWENTY-NINTH DAY

Intercessor in Heaven

Mary of Agreda tells us that the intercession of Saint Joseph is particularly most powerful: for attaining the virtue of purity and for overcoming the sensual inclinations of the flesh; for procuring powerful help to escape sin and return to the friendship of God; for increasing the love and devotion to most holy Mary; for inspiring the demons with terror at the mere mention of his name; for gaining health of body and assistance in all kinds of difficulties, and for securing issue of children in families.

She beseeches all the faithful children of the Church to be very devout to him, and they will experience these favors in reality, if they dispose themselves as they should, in order to receive and merit them.

In order to encourage great confidence in the intercession of Saint Joseph, St. Gertrude was granted the following vision:

"I saw Heaven opened and St. Joseph sitting upon a magnificent throne. I felt myself wonderfully affected when, each time his name was mentioned, all the saints made a profound inclination toward him showing that, by the serenity and sweetness of their looks, they rejoiced with him on account of his exalted dignity."

Dear Father St. Joseph, never cease recommending me, and the intention of this novena, to your Divine Son and your most Holy Spouse, Who are ever ready to grant your requests. +++

THIRTIETH DAY

Our Protector

St. Joseph has been solemnly proclaimed by Pope Pius IX as the "Patron and Protector of the Universal Church." And, although Saint Joseph is our father and advocate in all necessities, he is especially considered the Patron of a Happy Death, a provider for financial help—particularly to the poor and to religious communities—the patron of families, of laborers, of the sick, of the poor, of the rich (to help them distribute their possessions charitably and to help them attain the riches of Heaven), of the suffering, of travelers, of exiles, of the afflicted, of the married, of virgins, of youths, of priests and those aspiring to the priesthood, of those advanced in virtue, and those devoted to prayer.

He is also a rescuer of sinners, consoler and liberator of the Poor

Souls, terror of demons and conqueror of Hell. Pope Innocent XI made Saint Joseph the Patron of the Jesuit Missions in China, and Pope Pius XI proclaimed, "We place the vast campaign of the Church against world Communism under the standard of St. Joseph, her mighty protector.

Pope John Paul II adds that even today, we have perduring motives to recommend every man to Saint Joseph; his patronage is ever necessary for the Church, not only as a defense against all dangers that threaten her, but also, and indeed primarily, as an impetus for her renewed commitment to evangelization in the world, and re-evangelization in those lands and nations where religion and Christian life are now put to a hard test.

Dear Father St. Joseph, never cease recommending me, and the intention of this novena, to your Divine Son and your most Holy Spouse, Who are ever ready to grant your requests. +++

THIRTY-FIRST DAY

Dear Father St. Joseph

Saint Joseph was truly and fully a father...the most perfect of fathers. He received his mission from God, and was given authority over the Child. Authority is taken from the Latin word "augere," which means to make grow.

Saint Joseph is a role model who teaches that the contemplative and active life must be blended and harmonized, and that love is not the same as romantic daydreams, but must be enfleshed in a life of self-sacrifice and service to others that unfolds in the circumstances of the real world and in the profoundly human context of marriage and family.

Oh admirable Virgin! In the house at Nazareth, You, as well as Jesus, placed all Your glory and happiness in obeying Saint Joseph in all things; the slightest intimation of his wishes was a command in Your estimation; his will was the rule and guide of all Your actions, thoughts, and affections.

In short, it was Your highest ambition to descend to the lowest and most servile offices, in order to testify to Joseph the extent of that affection so justly due to the best of husbands; to show Your respect for so zealous and honorable a protector, and Your readiness to obey one whom You might well designate the most tender of fathers.

The secret of Saint Joseph's sanctity was his deep and constant devotion to God the Father. Fathers today might well turn to Saint Joseph as a ready and helpful advocate.

Dear Father St. Joseph, never cease recommending me, and the intention of this novena, to your Divine Son and your most Holy Spouse, Who are ever ready to grant your requests. +++

To You, O Blessed Joseph

(The new Enchiridion of Indulgences has, excepting ejaculations, just two items on St. Joseph: the Litany and the following prayer:)

To you, O blessed Joseph, do we come in our tribulation, and having implored the help of your most holy Spouse, we confidently invoke your patronage also. Through that charity which bound you to the Immaculate Virgin Mother of God, and through the paternal love with which you embraced the Child Jesus, we humbly beg you graciously to regard the inheritance which Jesus Christ has purchased by His Blood, and with your power and strength to aid us in our necessities.

O most watchful Guardian of the Holy Family, defend the chosen children of Jesus Christ; O most loving Father, ward off from us every contagion of error and corrupting influence; O our most mighty Protector, be propitious to us, and from Heaven assist us in our struggle with the power of darkness; and as once you rescued the Child Jesus from deadly peril, so now protect God's Holy Church from the snares of the enemy and from all adversity; shield, too, each one of us by your constant protection, so that supported by your example and your aid, we may be able to live piously, to die holily, and to obtain eternal happiness in Heaven. Amen. +++

75.

Litany of Saint Joseph

Lord, have mercy.
Christ, have mercy,
Lord, have mercy. Christ, hear us.
Christ graciously hears us.
God, the Father of Heaven,
have mercy on us.
God the Son, Redeemer of the world,
have mercy on us.
God the Holy Spirit,
have mercy on us.
Holy Trinity, One God,
have mercy on us.

Holy Mary,   (*pray for us.)*
St. Joseph,
Renowned Offspring of David,
Light of Patriarchs,
Spouse of the Mother of God,
Chaste Guardian of the Virgin,
Foster Father of the Son of God,
Diligent Protector of Christ,
Head of the Holy Family,
Joseph most just,
Joseph most chaste,
Joseph most prudent,
Joseph most strong,
Joseph most obedient,
Joseph most faithful,
Mirror of patience,
Lover of poverty,